Remember THIS

THINGS YOU ALREADY KNOW

WRITTEN BY: **M.H. CLARK**   DESIGNED BY: **SARAH FORSTER**

YOU KNOW THIS.

DEEP DOWN, YOU ALREADY KNOW THIS.
But sometimes, you forget. Sometimes, you need a reminder of the things you already know, because it's easy to lose sight of them. It's so easy to become distracted with the work of everyday living that the little voice that tells you the good things, the true things, the simple things, gets lost for a moment. Let this be your reminder. Let these words put you back on track. Let them speak to you. And let yourself believe them. Because they're powerful and they're true.

And you knew that already.

WHENEVER POSSIBLE, LOOK AT WHAT YOU HAVE AND **BE CONTENT.** *FEEL SATISFIED.* KNOW THAT, EVEN IF *JUST FOR THAT M O M E N T,* YOU HAVE **EVERYTHING.**

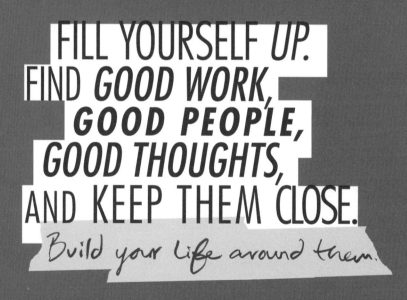

FILL YOURSELF *UP.*
FIND *GOOD WORK,*
GOOD PEOPLE,
GOOD THOUGHTS,
AND KEEP THEM CLOSE.
Build your life around them.

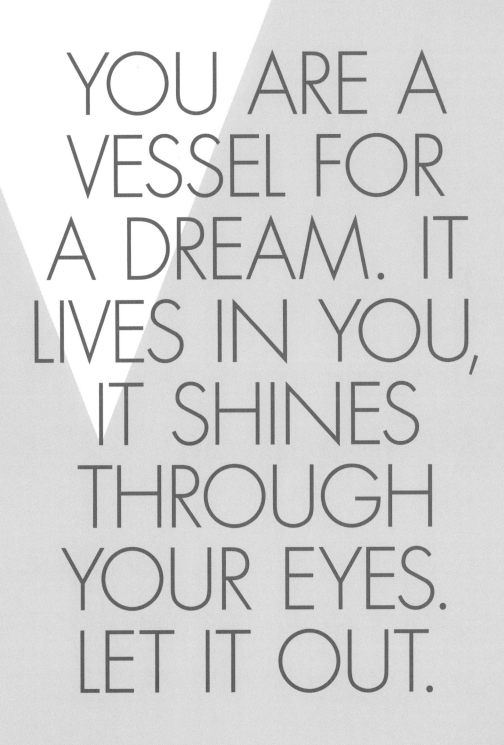

YOU ARE A VESSEL FOR A DREAM. IT LIVES IN YOU, IT SHINES THROUGH YOUR EYES. LET IT OUT.

OPPORTUNITIES ARE **EVERYWHERE**. THEY MAY BE *INVISIBLE*, THEY MAY BE *HARD TO IMAGINE* RIGHT NOW, BUT **THEY ARE *PRESENT*** AND THEY ARE *REAL*. **LOOK** FOR THEM.

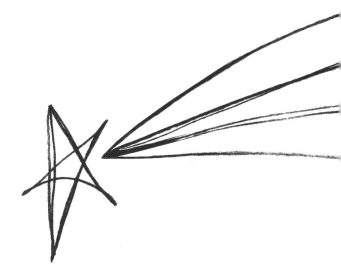

Your dreams are there to be listened to. THEY **DON'T** WANT TO BE TOLD THAT THEY'RE NOT REACHABLE; THEY **WANT** TO BE TOLD THAT YOU'LL FIND A WAY.

WHEN YOU LET GO
OF THE THINGS YOU *EXPECT,*
**YOU'LL DISCOVER ALL
THE *WONDERS*** YOU'VE
BEEN **SHUTTING OUT.**

EACH DAY IS AN *OPPORTUNITY* TO **MAKE A CHANGE,** *TO SHIFT DIRECTION,* TO COME A LITTLE CLOSER TO THE THINGS **YOUR HEART DESIRES.**

KEEP THE
PRESENT
PRESENT.
DO NOT
LOSE IT TO
PAST REGRET
OR FUTURE
WORRY.

NONE OF THIS IS *FOREVER.*

CHERISH
what should be cherished.

YOU HAVE *ENOUGH TIME* FOR ALL THE THINGS THAT **MATTER MOST.** AND IT IS UP TO *YOU* TO DISCOVER *WHAT* MATTERS MOST.

YOU ARE **THE ARCHITECT AND BUILDER** OF THIS DAY. *SHAPE IT WITH* **INTENTION.**

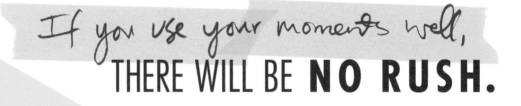

If you use your moments well,
THERE WILL BE **NO RUSH.**

Sometimes, IT WILL BE
NECESSARY TO DECIDE THAT
THERE ARE THINGS *YOU*
NO LONGER HAVE TIME FOR.

SLOW AND QUIET PROGRESS **IS PROGRESS, TOO.** *REMEMBER* TO GIVE YOURSELF CREDIT.

THE MORE YOU BELIEVE, THE MORE IS POSSIBLE.

THERE IS NO *DIRECT PATH*
TO THE PLACE YOU ARE GOING.
**YOU WILL HAVE TO
MAKE IT *YOURSELF.***

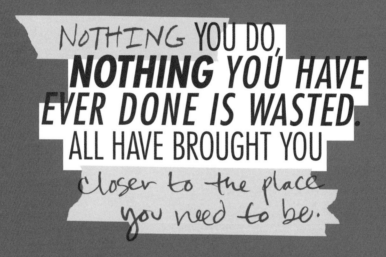

NOTHING YOU DO, **NOTHING** YOU HAVE EVER DONE IS WASTED. ALL HAVE BROUGHT YOU closer to the place you need to be.

MISTAKES DO
NOT MAKE
AN END.
THEY MAKE
ROOM FOR A
BEGINNING.

YOUR GIFT IS *NOT* IN
C O N F O R M I T Y.
YOUR GIFT IS IN THE
RARE AND ASTONISHING
THINGS THAT
ONLY YOU CAN OFFER.

PERFECTION
IS NOT WITHIN REACH.
LET IT GO.
FIND SOMETHING EVEN BETTER.

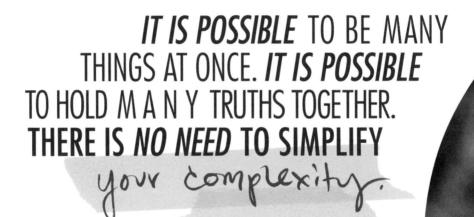

IT IS POSSIBLE TO BE MANY THINGS AT ONCE. *IT IS POSSIBLE* TO HOLD M A N Y TRUTHS TOGETHER. **THERE IS *NO NEED* TO SIMPLIFY** your complexity.

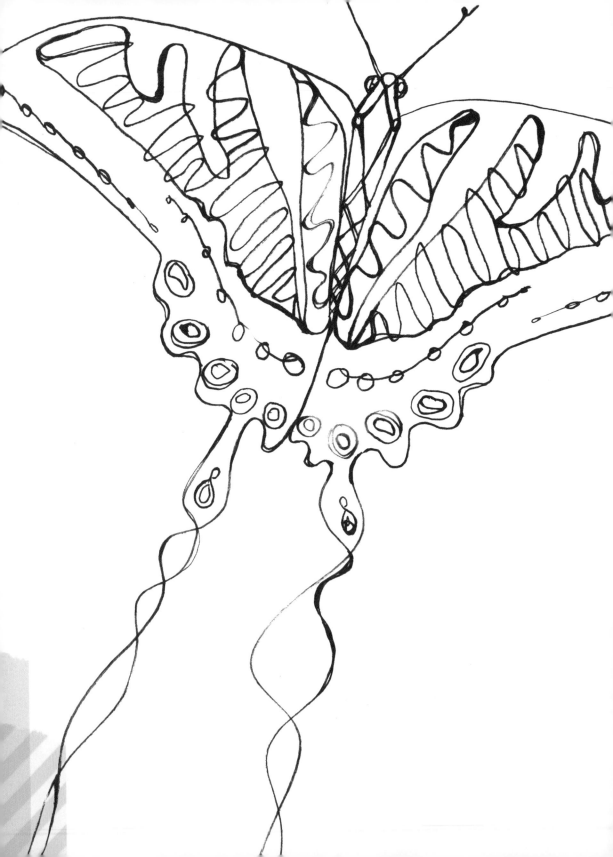

YOU ARE **COMPLETE**,
BUT YOU ARE NOT YET FINISHED.
DON'T STOP NOW.

YOUR TRUTH MATTERS.

Change is coming. AND IF *YOU* CANNOT CHOOSE WHAT HAPPENS, *YOU CAN CHOOSE* HOW YOU WILL REACT TO IT.

SOMETIMES, YOU NEED TO **GET OUT OF YOUR OWN WAY.** SOMETIMES, THE BIGGEST OBSTACLE YOU FACE IS *YOURSELF.*

KEEP DOING WHATEVER
ENGAGES *YOUR MIND.*
KEEP FOLLOWING WHATEVER
ENGAGES *YOUR HEART.*

IT TAKES A LOT TO LIVE. IT'S STILL WORTH IT.

HAPPINESS IS *ALWAYS* A **CHOICE.**

The journey matters, too.
FIND A WAY TO **LOVE** THE ROAD *YOU'RE ON.*

WHAT YOU
CAN CHANGE
IS THE PART
THAT IS YOURS.
ONLY THE PART
THAT IS YOURS.

THIS MAY BE *JUST THE LESSON YOU DIDN'T KNOW YOU NEEDED.* THE ONE THAT **ALTERS EVERYTHING.**

A DETOUR
DOES NOT MEAN YOU ARE BEING STOPPED.
IT MAY MEAN YOU ARE BEING
REROUTED, *REDIRECTED,*
CHALLENGED.

Seek another way.

THERE ARE *SEASONS OF WAITING* AND **SEASONS OF GROWTH.** IF YOU AREN'T GROWING NOW, *GET READY.* **YOU WILL.**

The world will **CHANGE YOU,** *SHAPE YOU,* AND DEFINE YOU.

REMEMBER TO **CHANGE,** *SHAPE,* AND DEFINE THE WORLD.

IF YOU CAN FIND **SOMETHING** *TO BE GRATEFUL FOR* IN THIS **M O M E N T**, *WHEREVER YOU ARE*, YOU HAVE FOUND A SHORTCUT TO **HAPPINESS.**

Always keep AT LEAST **ONE WISH** THAT IS *BIGGER THAN YOU ARE.*

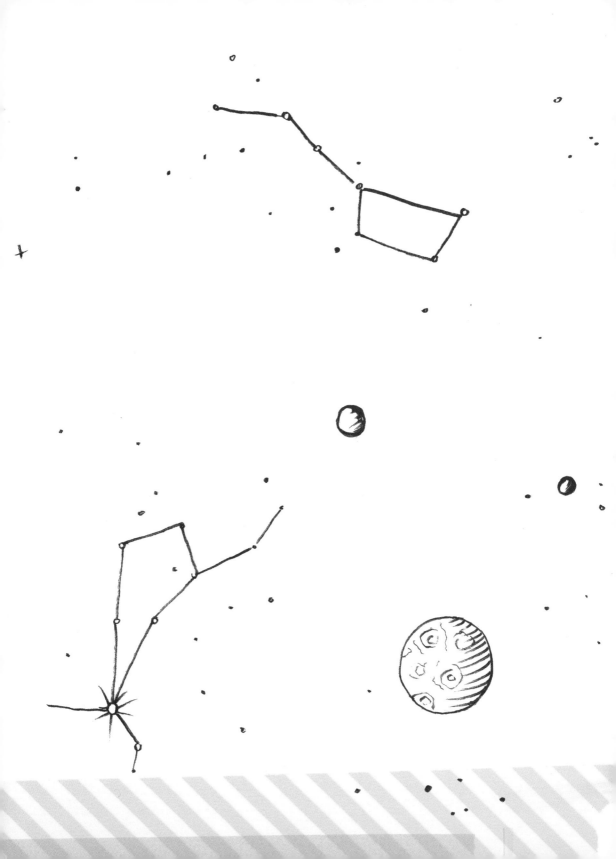

THERE IS MORE
JOY COMING.

YOU MIGHT BE THE
VERY THING
YOU'RE LOOKING FOR.

COMPENDIUM®
live inspired.

WITH *SPECIAL THANKS* TO THE **ENTIRE** COMPENDIUM FAMILY.

CREDITS:

WRITTEN BY: **M.H. CLARK**

DESIGNED BY: **SARAH FORSTER**

EDITED BY: **AMELIA RIEDLER**

CREATIVE DIRECTION BY: **JULIE FLAHIFF**

PHOTOGRAPHY BY: FRONT AND BACK COVER: JYESHERN CHENG / E+ / GETTY IMAGES; PAGES 2–5: SUSCHAA / PHOTOCASE.COM; PAGES 10–11: TI.NA / PHOTOCASE.COM; PAGES 10–12: ISTOCKPHOTO / THINKSTOCK; PAGES 16–17: GRÄFIN. / PHOTOCASE.COM; PAGES 20–21: SUSCHAA / PHOTOCASE.COM; PAGES 24–25: THINKSTOCK; PAGES 26–28: [PHOTOGRAPHY MAKES ME HAPPY} / FLICKR SELECT / GETTY IMAGES; PAGES 34–35: CYOOH / PHOTOCASE.COM; PAGES 40–41: JUPITERIMAGES / THINKSTOCK; PAGES 44–47: JENZIG71 / PHOTOCASE.COM; PAGES 50–54: VIOLESS / PHOTOCASE.COM; PAGES 60–61: LKPRO / PHOTOCASE.COM; PAGES 67–69: CYOOH / PHOTOCASE.COM; PAGES 72–74: ©ISTOCKPHOTO.COM / PAILOOLOM; PAGES 78–80: RAPERONZOLO / PHOTOCASE.COM.

ISBN: 978-1-938298-08-0

2ND PRINTING. PRINTED IN CHINA WITH SOY INKS.